The Money Matrix Method™

How To Quickly and Easily Condition Your Mind For *Massive* Success!

by **Michael Craig**
Author of *The Logical Soul*®

Publisher's Data & Legal Information

ISBN 978-0-9800674-7-7
Published by Logical Soul LLC
6050 Peachtree Parkway, 240-340, Norcross, GA 30092
For support, contact publisher@logicalsoul.com
Layout & Index by Michael Craig
Cover by Gaurav Sikka

Every attempt has been made by the author to acknowledge the sources used for the material in this book. If there has been any omission, please contact the publisher at the email given.

ABOUT THE AUTHOR

MICHAEL CRAIG has found the key to happiness. He is married to a beautiful woman who loves him, works in a sunlit office at home in a business he loves, rides a unicycle for health and fun, travels for relaxation at least twice a year, earns (with his wife) a six-figure income, and is debt-free.

He didn't always know success, however. As the son of a struggling middle-class couple, he learned early in life that money troubles were simply the way of the world. Although he instinctively fought this idea, and spent most of his adult life working on his "money issues," nothing seemed to work. Money problems persisted.

He was divorced twice, bankrupt, and drifted in and out of businesses, and from job to job. Some success came, followed by the inevitable crash. Driven to learn what held him back over and over again, Michael tens of thousands of dollars traveling the world for courses and gurus to learn the secrets to health, wealth, and happiness. While some of his efforts bore fruit, it took years of self-discovery and inward reflection to discover the real key to success.

Then it took another twenty years of testing himself and others until he finally perfected a method of *eliminating* the painful ups and downs regarding money, wealth and happiness. Michael was able to develop an easy and effective way to incorporate both ancient and modern techniques, and the **Logical Soul**® and **The Money Matrix Method**™ are the results of this work.

Dr. Craig lives in the Atlanta area. He is a host for a weekly Blog Talk Radio program called *Logical Soul*® *Talk*, blogs, sees private clients, and gives presentations to various groups and forums. He may be reached via email found on his website at www.moneymatrixmethod.com.

To Soma

To my teachers and mentors
To my ancestors
To my readers

May you find happiness and satisfaction
in knowing you helped me write these words.

TESTIMONIALS

"It's totally law of attraction, it's totally responsibility; it's totally taking charge of your life. I love it . . . We're in perfect resonance! I'm yours; you got me at 'hello'!"
- Raymond Aaron
Author, *Double Your Income Doing What You Love*
www.MonthlyMentorReview.com

"In my years of hanging around successful people long enough to become one myself, I'm convinced that you absolutely need both an INTENSE DESIRE and EXTREME FOCUS in order to achieve the success you deserve and desire. This book helps unlock these secrets and is a definite MUST READ!"
- Devon Brown, "The Success Renegade"
www.RenegadeSuccess.com

"I have been working on my inner issues for years and never came across anything like what Michael presents here. The Money Matrix Method™ is totally unique. It opened my eyes to inner blocks I could never have imagined before!"
- Ronda del Boccio, "The Story Lady"
www.ProfitableStorytelling.com

"I feel great . . . I feel a tremendous amount of energy and relief. Your work is very powerful!"
- Dr. Brenda Wade
TV Psychologist, author and Keynote Speaker
www.loveandmoneysummit.com

"Michael you've definitely hit the nail on the head with The Money Matrix Method™! *The techniques you recommend are pure genius, and I'm already envisioning the many lives that will be positively impacted by your insights!"*
- Jason Oman
#1 Best-Selling Author,
Conversations with Millionaires.
www.conversationswithmillionaires.com

"I've read, watched, and listened to a lot of personal development content over the years. Also, I've attended many personal development events that were empowering, but Dr. Craig's work incorporates all the strategies and techniques into one book. I love how Michael makes implementing these life changing techniques easy. This is an excellent book for anyone ready to make a life change, today!"
C.F. Jackson
Author / Consultant, Atlanta, Georgia
www.WebsiteMakeoverWorkshop.com

TABLE OF CONTENTS

VIII

FOREWORD

After years of studying and spending time with various self-made millionaires, I achieved a certain degree of success myself. I was a Featured Success Story on a TV infomercial called *Creating Wealth* and then followed that up by creating my #1 Best-Selling book *Conversations with Millionaires* in 2001. More recently I completed *Conversations with Female Millionaires* and plan to launch other related products and services in the near future. As a result of my unique associations and endeavors I can tell you that the secrets revealed in this book – *The Money Matrix Method*™ – can truly help you create incredible wealth and success!

From the years I've been studying the wealthy, I've become aware of the considerable gap between their state of mind and the mind of those yet to attain wealth. While there are all sorts of theories and solutions out there, I've yet to see the kind of mental/emotional changes that can happen to someone's mindset as I've seen demonstrated using *The Money Matrix Method*™. It simply works!

The Money Matrix Method™ can not only help you identify the speed bumps or roadblocks holding you back from the results you desire, but best of all it can even help you *eliminate* those roadblocks so you can finally achieve your goals and make your dreams come true!

For years Michael Craig has worked with folks to help raise their money consciousness. I've seen him achieve phenomenal results after just one or two sessions. A woman I know personally expanded her possibilities and earning potential by *over 50 times* over what she previously had after a very short time. And, while this is a long way from actually achieving tangible results, the initial mindset shifts I noticed were amazing.

I believe the *Money Matrix Method*™ to be totally unique. It stands on its own as incomparable to anything else you'll find in the success marketplace out there. Best of all, it can help you finally break through and get into the 'FLOW' that can cause amazing success to happen!

I believe if you take action on the information contained in this book, you will achieve levels of success far beyond anything you've ever even imagined was possible. It simply takes the right focus and action. Do what this book says and success can be YOURS!

Start now. Focus and take action *today* and learn *The Money Matrix Method*™. You won't regret it!

Jason Oman
#1 Best-Selling Author
www.ConversationsWithMillionaires.com
www.ConversationsWithFemaleMillionaires.com

CHAPTER ONE

What's a "Money Matrix"?

There is nothing scarier than the thought of REALLY making a lot of Money. Wealth is scary. Success is frightening. And abundance is, let's face it . . . downright *unnatural.*

I'm not the only one saying things like this. **Marianne Williamson** was even quoted by Nelson Mandela in his presidential inaugural speech:

> *"Our deepest fear is not that we are inadequate. Our deepest fear is that we are powerful beyond measure. It is our light, not our darkness that most frightens us."*

Oh, sure . . . you are probably fond of *SAYING* you want more money, more success, and more wealth. But when it comes right down to it, total success frightens you beyond measure. You have *VERY GOOD REASONS* why you aren't rich, can't get rich, or shouldn't <u>be</u> rich.

You SAY you want money, but deep down you FEEL you don't. Believe it or not, this is by design. <u>There is an underlying LOGIC to the whole process.</u> This network of confused beliefs, hidden and conscious decisions, thoughts, and ideas about money, wealth, and our relationship to both is called the **Money Matrix.**

This matrix is also the web of attitudes and decisions about money and wealth that lies within you, as well as *the foundation for all your expressions* about money and wealth. Expressed more simply:

> Your **Money Matrix** is your *capacity* to attract money and wealth. This matrix is also the entire field of awareness held together by hidden decisions that determine your views and attitudes of money and wealth throughout your life.

This matrix has been locked away from your conscious awareness ever since you were too young to know what was happening. It is, therefore, extremely difficult to access and change.

While some people have had success in "re-programming" this matrix, most have found it difficult, if not impossible, to affect a permanent change. It is a curious fact that, like fingerprints or DNA, your money matrix usually stays the same throughout your life.

No matter what your background, if you have a wealth-oriented matrix, you become wealthy. If you have a poverty-oriented matrix, the acquisition or retention of money becomes a lifelong struggle. But why is that?

Money Matrix as a Fruit Bowl

When you normally think of re-programming the mind, what comes to mind? Most likely *words, suggestion, affirmations, statements, hypnosis, NLP,* or *inner subconscious commands.* While each of these factors produce some results, they are akin to the *CONTENT* of our minds, i.e., the "fruit" in a "bowl of fruit." The *fruit* is the *content* – the "stuff" in the bowl.

Your money matrix, however, is much more basic. It is the <u>*CONTEXT*</u> of your mind, i.e., <u>*HOW*</u> you actually hold the views of the world around you. In our bowl of fruit analogy, the money matrix is more closely tied into the **BOWL.**

While the *mind itself* is the bowl, the matrix might determine, for example, the *shape, color,* and *texture* of this bowl, <u>*NOT*</u> the words or programs (i.e., content) contained within it.

This is a very important distinction.

A wealthy person – just like anyone else - may experience some financial difficulties in his or her life. But these difficulties do not run their lives. A money matrix set on "wealth" means that this person has firmly established wealth on the *inside* . . . even if it takes some time to unfold on the *outside.* A person with a matrix set on "wealthy" owns the DRIVE to succeed, and the matrix – and universe - will make sure this happens!

Also, wealth-oriented people do *NOT understand how non-wealthy people can stay broke.* They don't see the hidden tether that binds non-wealth-matrix people to poverty or lack.

How to Train an Elephant

The way they train elephants in Thailand, Burma or Sri Lanka is very simple: they tie a rope around the fellow's leg at a very young age, and tether it to a stake in the ground. He is not yet very large, so he cannot escape. He is grounded to that spot.

Later in life, when the elephant is fully grown, this rope and stake continue to serve as a prison for this giant. Despite the fact that a 2-ton elephant can EASILY uproot the rope and stake at any time, HE NEVER TRIES! The elephant has been trained since early childhood that the rope is UNBREAKABLE!! You might say his "freedom matrix" is set for "stay put."

Some people are trained since childhood to develop a unique wealth matrix. One friend and associate who is also a best-selling author, was trained by his mother at a very early age to expect a greater and greater reward each year. Consequently, his money matrix is consistently wealth-oriented . . . and the results almost always follow.

How to Train a Human

"But," you might ask, "I didn't have that upbringing. Now what?"

Often a counselor, psychologist or therapist might recommend you "work on your money issues" until you get clear of the "limiting beliefs" you have. You didn't have the advantage of wealth-conscious parents, so "re-programming" is necessary . . .

Hogwash.

If you're like me, you've already been there and done that. You've just tried "re-programming your subconscious mind." You've cranked up the affirmations, hypnosis, subliminal tapes, willpower and NLP. You've re-aligned your chakras, and re-discovered your inner child. You proclaimed the release of all negative influences in your life. You meditated hours a day, surrounded yourself with loving, supportive people, and tried to follow your passion.

But you're still broke, right?

Now don't get me wrong . . . there _are_ ways to effectively change your conditioning, but not by using the same old "re-programming" methods. Treating our minds these days has not advanced much beyond our knowledge of health over 200 years ago. At that time, "bleeding" was thought to be the best method to "balance the humours" and bring about good health. But it seldom worked, and often killed the patient.

While "re-programming" is understood not to be as dangerous as bleeding, it also is NOT the answer. The subconscious mind is a powerful being inside of us. It knows all our tricks. It also has a *very good reason* to keep things just the way they are. While you may fool it once or twice, it seldom gets fooled for long.

So what's the answer, if not re-programming??

The Right Way: Conditioning

Conditioning is the word I use to describe the process of **connecting** with our subconscious self and **communicating** our desires. This process does *NOT* involve trying to force new programming on a subconscious "thing." This is a fairly radical concept, and I'll cover it later in this chapter.

For right now, it's enough for you to know that, just as others came from seemingly-insurmountable circumstances to wealth, so can you. *Conditioning* is a way to address the condition of the BOWL, not endlessly try to rearrange (or reprogram, or analyze) the fruit.

You've probably heard the success stories: a young John Rockefeller, Andrew Carnegie, and Henry Ford built empires from scratch . . . and immigrants like Arnold Schwarzenegger who came from humble beginnings to make millions. Stories like these and others suggest the American Dream is still available to anyone willing to work hard and provide value to others.

However these stories, while inspirational, often fail to point out that, like my author friend who *also* came from humble beginnings, it's the *DIRECTION towards incremental success* in one's early years that lead them to develop a success matrix, *NOT* the *amount* of one's success.

A **consistent movement towards achievement** in one's early life – even if it is very small – establishes a solid wealth-oriented money matrix that leads to consistent success as an adult.

You've hear the expression "Nothing succeeds like success." This is true. If you don't have a foundation for this success, however, you must create it – INSIDE your mind and heart first!

Had the baby elephant in my last example been given the freedom in his early years to go further and further on the rope, and taught to actually BREAK the rope at some point, he would naturally develop a strong *"freedom matrix."* But the vested interests of the owners are at stake, so he's never shown how.

Like that, parents and elders have vested interests. Whether they are conscious of them or not, most parents will say "no" to their child, not only because of fear for the child's safety and well-being, but also because they were told "no" themselves! This heritage of limitation usually passes from generation to generation to generation.

Conditioning the mind is a way to set up the circumstances where inner limitations can be known, then brand new matrix decisions made. The first step is to bump into your own *Money Matrix* and discover whether or not it is set on *"poor!"* If so, you know it is part of a protective layer of what you know as your reality. And it rarely changes.

You can no more "fix" your matrix than you can "fix" your fingerprints or eye color! This does NOT mean, however, that you cannot alter the **hidden factors** WITHIN the Matrix and see some powerful results.

The Money Matrix Method™

Changing the money matrix cannot be changed using military-style tactics like a frontal assault (in-your-face "scared straight" therapy), a flanking maneuver (hypnosis, NLP, EFT, tapping, bodywork), or by negotiating from a weakened or inferior position (goals, affirmations). In fact, *you can't change the Money Matrix at all!*

But this does not mean the problem is unsolvable. It only means that your usual approaches have been ineffective! A wise person once said:

> **"You can't solve a problem on the level of the problem."**

Money problems usually have a very deep and mysterious origin. You see, you may be among the majority of people who go about addressing these problems all wrong. You may not know, for example, that your lack of money has *nothing to do with money itself,* but in the **relationships** around money! Once you open the flow to these hidden relationships, *Voila!* . . . . your relationship to money changes!

It took me over 20 years to discover that . . .

> a) there was in fact a hidden "money matrix,"
> b) this matrix had its own innate logic or intelligence, and
> c) there were hidden links that allowed it to change.

I called it **The Money Matrix Method**™ and developed it to be completely different from existing therapies and approaches. Here are some of the comparisons:

The Money Matrix Method™ **is** *NOT* . . .

> ➢ Hypnosis, NLP, EFT, Tapping, etc.
> ➢ Repetitious Affirmations
> ➢ Goal Setting
> ➢ Willpower or "efforting"
> ➢ Some special technique done by a doctor or practitioner, or
> ➢ Any technique that tries to fool the subconscious mind.

What the Money Matrix Method™ *IS* . . .

> ➢ Easy to Learn and Use
> ➢ Natural
> ➢ Can be practiced by anyone

➢ Based on the natural tendencies of the mind
➢ Based on both conscious and subconscious feedback
➢ Based on the entire spectrum of personal experience
➢ Effective in both form and results

The *Money Matrix Method*™ provides you with an effective way to FIND, ACCESS and CHANGE deep-rooted (subconscious) factors or *matrix decisions* about money. These decisions are like circuit breakers. They can either turn ON – or turn OFF – your connection to money, your self-worth, and your ability to receive, use, and appreciate money and what it can do.

Most of these hidden matrix decisions were made way back when you were very young. However, *some money decisions are not even your own,* but are inherited from parents, ancestors, friends, relatives and others.

In order to get access to these hidden matrix decisions, most of which were made before you could even talk, you must be able to access what I call your "subconscious self" or "inner child." **This "self" remembers everything.** It never forgets *any decision you've ever made.*

The *Money Matrix Method*™ uses self-questioning and simple muscle-testing to "flip the circuit breaker" and change these decisions. While techniques like NLP, hypnosis, or therapy may give you relief, they often cannot address core issues simply because you (or the therapist) *may miss the key subconscious elements entirely!*

Consequently, such approaches to therapy are an attempt to "pave over the swamp" by trying to trick your subconscious mind into believing something that runs counter to its *own* hidden "laws" about money. This almost never works long-term. There needs to be a consensus between your inner and outer "selves" on how to tap into this vast inner power you have – and *how to express it!*

This Book will reveal:

- **The Success Sabotage Syndrome,** *and how it forms,*
- **Your most Urgent Needs:** *What you REALLY want, as opposed to what you THINK you want,*
- **7 Powerful Statements,** *and what they mean to you,*
- **How to Discover the #1 Factor** *that affects your capacity for wealth,*
- **"Mind Viruses"** *or patterns of hidden matrix decisions that lock you into severe limitation – and how to escape them, and*
- **How to Discover What You Love** *and how to turn your passion into a successful business or income!*

Real Wealth comes from within, not imposed by affirmations, or by following some rich guru, book, or success course. Once you tap into your own personal *Money Matrix* (complex of hidden wealth decisions) you will *just know.* That's the beauty of the whole process – it's all about YOU, not some universal "law" or "secret."

CHAPTER TWO

Success Sabotage Syndrome

Where's the Money?

Whether or not they admit it, many people measure both happiness and success by the amount of money they make. I know I did, and that's why I wasn't very happy for many years. According to what **T. Harv Eker's** assessment might be, my "money thermostat" was set very low.

"Wealth consciousness," believe it or not, has much more to do with **RELATIONSHIPS** than it does about money. Your relationship with yourself, primarily. Then there is the relationship with your Mom and Dad, or your spouse or significant other. Relationships with prospects, customers, suppliers, society, family, ancestors, and even the relationship to money itself . . . all play a part in this thing called "the Money Matrix."

But it all starts with you. If you are a woman, you may want money to feel secure or creative. If you are a man, you might need money to feel powerful, sexy, free, comfortable and capable of supporting your family. These are all laudable goals. So _why don't you have the money you so desperately need and want?!_

I have a theory based on years and years of observation and personal experience that I call **Success Sabotage Syndrome,** and it goes like this:

> You are not wealthy because the *matrix* *decisions* related to getting, earning or attracting wealth are superseded by deeper survival or tribal needs.

"Success" is defined differently by your subconscious mind than by your conscious mind! If you are unaware of – or ignore - this fact, you will regularly *subconsciously sabotage all your attempts to make or keep money!* Then you fool ourselves into thinking that the problem lies somewhere else.

Self-Sabotage Syndrome is a self-delusion comes full circle when you think you must work harder and harder doing the same old things. Your rationale is that you'll eventually break through and have that money you need so much.

But you never do . . . and yet you keep trying. Einstein's definition of insanity (doing the same things over and over while expecting different results) keeps you stuck on the mouse wheel going nowhere except deeper into debt.

How do I know this? Growing up I had a severe case of Self-Sabotage Syndrome. I was the Charlie-Brown-type, always running to kick the football. And, true-to-life, someone was always there to "pull a Lucy on me" and yank it away at the last minute.

Over the years I willingly engaged in this self-deception in order to "win" this cosmic game called life. And I usually ended up losing it all.

In the mid-1980's, for example, I was looking for answers after a series of major personal crises occurred that left me heart-broken and penniless. I found relief in positive motivation seminars, books and tapes . . . a path to finally achieving my goals.

What I *actually achieved,* however, was far short of what I hoped for. Affirmations. Positive thinking. NLP. Tapping. The Law of Attraction. The Secret. All of these ideas and techniques made perfect sense to me, and I read and practiced them religiously . . . but also stayed broke.

Although I could point to the occasional "money miracle" that showed up in my life, I was hard-pressed to understand that "manifesting" money and things were no substitute for the accumulation of *real* wealth. It took me another 20 years to get off the "Hope" bandwagon and discover my OWN hidden laws about money . . . the ones I *inherited* from a long line of ancestors with the same money challenges. In the process, I discovered how these "personal laws" - or hidden money decisions - ran my life.

Now don't get me wrong. I'm *NOT* saying that affirmations, the Law of Attraction, etc., have no value for you. Quite the contrary. These teachings are chock full of wisdom and value, and have been for ages.

The problem is, *few people know how to actually USE this wisdom.* Just like a third-grader might understand the basic idea behind Einstein's equation $E=mc^2$ if explained properly, I doubt there are any who could tell me how to put together a nuclear reactor!

Like that, the **Law of Attraction** is thrown around as some universal solution to everyday problems. Most of those who use it, however, do not have the psychological tools necessary to discover their own *hidden agendas* and *relationship cutoffs.* They don't realize that, in order to reap benefits from the Law of Attraction, they must convert seed ideas into *focused brain and body activity* that results in money. And this takes a high degree of self-knowledge and understanding.

While a few success "gurus" are born with these innate tools, most are not. Consequently, the gurus say it's all very simple. While it may be for them, the rest of humanity exhibits way too many gaps between their thinking, action and results.

Money Blind Spots

You have blind spots when it comes to money. This "split mind" keeps you constantly at war with yourself . . . *and you don't see it!*

Both your Conscious (ego) AND Subconscious minds (id) must be in alignment when it comes to money and success, creating an *INNER KNOWING* and *CONVICTION.* When this happens, money and success will naturally flow towards you.

Probably 95% of those who use *Law of Attraction* techniques or teachings don't get this. You want to get rich quick. You want instant goodies. You might even think you are just lazy or don't try hard enough – not knowing that this has very little to do with your inaction!

Like a freshman in high school, you may religiously follow the FORM of the instructions, but not understand the hidden rules that bring about real results. You don't realize the subconscious mind (or right brain) is concerned most about **relationships** and survival at all costs. If this means holding on to poverty consciousness 'til death do us part, then by golly . . . *it will do that!* And it has a *good reason* for holding on, as you will see later.

The fact that you don't know this *consciously* doesn't matter. You are still held hostage by a force that demands survival and links to things seemingly beyond your control. Meanwhile, you may keep thinking you are "sabotaging yourself" and try to fix it.

There is an easier way of seeing this "money thing" . . .

How to Manifest Anything

"Manifesting money" is not really a mystery. You have a thought, then a desire, then take action leading (hopefully) to fulfillment. Making money is, in fact, a very straightforward process, as shown in the following diagram:

HOW IT *SHOULD* BE . . .

You start with a THOUGHT and end up with FULFILLMENT. Simple, huh?

The world of WEALTH FULFILMENT is populated by those I call *"The Great Ones."* These are the Tony Robbinses, Robert Kyosakis and Oprah Winfreys we all know and love. The Great Ones have learned to master this cycle by first becoming solidly aligned with their real **intent.**

They naturally **focus** on what they want and conceive of owning it *right now,* not months or years later.

They also have relationships that support making and attracting money. This does NOT mean, by the way, that the relationships *themselves* are healthy. It only means that the MONEY MATRIX is set on high.

The above is NOT how it works for most of humanity, however. The *"Self-Sabotage Syndrome Cycle"* is more complicated. In fact, most people go through *quite a few* complicated steps in trying to be wealthy, but predictably arrive instead at heartache and disappointment.

HOW IT *REALLY* IS . . .

Being:
UNFUL-
FILLED

THOUGHT

DESIRE
+
HIDDEN
DECISION

STOP
ACTION OR
SELF-
SABOTAGE

SELF-SABOTAGE SYNDROME CYCLE

ACTION
WITH
HIDDEN
AGENDA

MIXED
INTENT

Your original desire for success becomes diluted with *pre-existing,* **hidden matrix decisions (HMDs)** and attitudes given you by family, ancestors and authority figures that have very little to do with money. These hidden decisions are based on subconscious priorities that were in place *before* your desire for money.

Believe it or not, this is the *NORM!* And it's complicated and depressing. You don't *want* to look at it . . . that's why the decisions are hidden! These same decisions, however, affect you. Your INTENT becomes diluted and your desired RESULTS are either sabotaged or distorted.

So what do you do? You set out to learn all about the *Law of Attraction* and *The Secret,* then hope you can AFFIRM your way out of this mess.

The only problem is, you usually over-simplify your ability to "manifest," and base it on your earliest ability, i.e., a belief in SANTA CLAUSE (or something similar like "Spirit"). At one time in your life, you asked for something . . . *and it was given to you!* You may not have known *HOW* it showed up. You only know it *did*!

This inner training lead you to embrace **"The Santa Clause Theory of Reality."** While this is great for kids, it is deadly for adults. Yet your wealth thinking still operates on this thing called "hope."

HOW YOU *HOPE* IT IS . . .

Desire  **Results**

Many people (subconsciously at least) *still think this way as adults!!* Deep down, you're still waiting for Santa Claus to show up.

But he doesn't. Neither do those things you tried to manifest. Why? You didn't understand – or allow for – the NORMAL CYCLE to unfold. Your hidden agendas based on the low settings in your *Money Matrix* got you every time!

In the next chapter, I will reveal some RULES to help you understand how - and WHY – this split takes place. After that, you will have a firm grasp on what needs to be done if you want to reach that Holy Grail . . . SUCCESS!

CHAPTER THREE

Rules of the Money Matrix

There are four (4) **Rules of the Money Matrix.** Most successful people know these rules intuitively. Here's #1:

RULE #1
The Law of Attraction only works when the core <u>inner</u> beliefs and decisions are in alignment with the <u>outer</u> ones.

Sounds like a simple Law of Attraction formula, right? Actually, it's much more complicated than that. For instance, how do you go about changing an inner belief if it is based on a perceived *survival* need . . . or a need that is *a higher priority* than your stated goal?

How do you achieve your goal of becoming rich, for example, when your family all have long-held beliefs that "rich people are dishonest"...? Most of us, when faced with such subtle tribal or family pressure would simply avoid wealth *subconsciously*, while telling ourselves *consciously* that we still want wealth!

So, rather than addressing such a complex issue, you may prefer instead to simply assume your inner wiring is a bit faulty. You then try to "program" it into going along with what the conscious idea of you want, i.e., to be rich!

The result? Sometimes it works; most of the time it doesn't. But is this your fault?

No.

Let's face it: when it comes to self-development we are *ALL* in the third grade! The self-development movement is, in fact, less than a hundred years old. It started when **Charles F. Haanel,** a self-made businessman and the "father" of the movement, discovered and first wrote about the law of attraction in 1912 in *The Master Key System.*

In this book, Haanel outlined 24 Lessons that were designed to take us from "poverty consciousness" to wealth in short order. Since then, books like *Think and Grow Rich* and others have fed us a steady diet of you-can-do-it-if-you-believe-it advice.

Again, while this advice works well for the few whose *money matrices* are already set on "go," the majority simply don't get it. Most human beings must dig for something a little deeper within themselves. How deep? It depends...

Maslow's Hierarchy of Needs

In 1943, psychologist **Abraham Maslow** published his "Theory of Motivation" which contained, among other things, reference to a "hierarchy of needs."

Maslow postulated that we have different layers of needs – each layer dependant on the one before it. If, for example, you were dying of thirst in the desert and somebody offered you a glass of water for $100,000, you would have no trouble paying it (assuming you HAD the money on you)!

Like that, Maslow's layers were set up to where each layer became the foundation for the one above it. Survival first, then safety, then friendship . . . all the way up to what he called *"self-actualization."* The last item was a state of personal self-sufficiency where happiness is the predominant emotion.

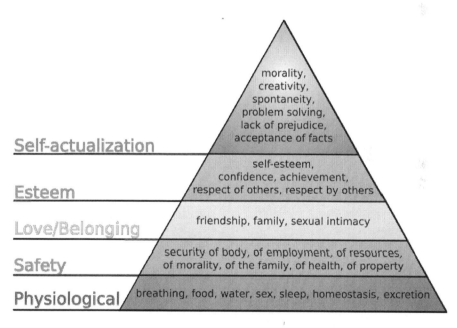

Image source: http://en.wikipedia.org

The needs in Maslow's hierarchy are usually self-evident. Given a choice between satisfying the desire to follow one's passion (level 5) or eating (level 1), most sane people will choose the latter.

Its only when the need for food is satisfied does the need to have other things arise. Until then, primary needs control.

"Jumping higher" within the pyramid does not work. While you may WANT to achieve great things, your subconscious mind will always choose the more basic needs first. If you try to skip a level, the result is difficulty, self-sabotage or failure.

How You Sabotage Your Success

In my own quest to make money, I experienced a very real innate stubbornness. There was a hidden part of me that steadfastly held onto my ideas and comfort zone, *even if that meant giving up my financial goals!*

Incredible? I thought so too. This power was SO strong within me that it rendered effective action almost impossible. This is the *Success Sabotage Syndrome* I described in the previous chapter, and apparently *everyone with money issues is faced with it.*

This syndrome is present in those who have a basic need that has <u>NOT</u> been met, according to Maslow's Hierarchy. Nor has this need been acknowledged; it usually has been pushed very far down into the subconscious mind until all conscious memory of it has vanished.

RULE #2

Until your most basic needs are acknowledged and resolved you will find it difficult to achieve your money goals. Your *Prime Directive* is to address those needs first.

So what are your most basic needs? How do you find and satisfy them? Shelter? Food? Love or acceptance from parents?? Whatever it is, just know that THIS is your quest above all other superficial concerns, including money.

> *(NOTE: There appears to be an exception to Rule #2, i.e., when your money goal is having enough to survive. This actually proves the rule, however, by ACKNOWLEDGING your need bring in enough money or resources to survive!)*

Once you can re-set your hidden subconscious decisions to work <u>with</u> your conscious money goals instead of <u>against</u> them, you will become a living powerhouse. Like magic, people and resources will show up that launch you to almost instant success!

The Law of Human Reality

How do you interact with the world? Do you feel responsible for everything that happens? Or do you feel more like a victim?

If you are a struggling victim, there is only one thing I would suggest to you: try on the idea of **being responsible** for everything around you.

Once you do you are ready for RULE #3. If you don't feel ready to take on this belief, just TRY it on, like you would a new coat or pair of pants. Even if the idea doesn't feel right, try it on. Humor me; you won't be sorry. Ready?

RULE #3
Your world IS what you decide - inside.

This is like that New Age admonition *"The world is as you are"* <u>with one critical difference</u>. I added "inside" because I'm not simply talking about *conscious* decisions. It's your *hidden ones* that either support or sabotage your success!

The Law of The Very Good Reason

RULE #4: *If we are not successful, deep down we have a very good reason <u>NOT</u> to succeed!*

What is your REASON for having money? What are your stated money dreams?

Here are some examples people gave:

> *"I choose to have enough money to support myself and my family very comfortably."*

> *"I choose wealth so that I can give more generously to charity."*

> *"I choose to be a millionaire so I can make a difference in the world."*

> *"I choose a fancy car, the house on the beach, the time to spend with my family, and the ability to travel the world."*

Great and noble reasons . . . but probably none of these are the real reasons.   How do I know? Testing. Years and years of testing.

Reality Check: Are you on the path to actually *DOING* something about any of these dreams? If so, congratulations.

If you are like most people, however, you are living on some future dream that somewhere, somehow, your ship will come in? Digging deeper, you will find *you don't have a sufficient reason.*

If you've ever come close to drowning or suffocating, you know that the ONLY desire you have at the moment is a breath of air! Many wealthy people say their desire for wealth was like that.

Don't have a desire for wealth that strong? Then find it! Matrix Rule #4 also implies that, unless you have a *GOOD ENOUGH REASON* to have money, it won't come to you. This reason must be powerful enough to move you to dynamic action!

All too often, though, the *opposite* is true: too many people have very deep (and "good enough") reasons to AVOID money and wealth!

Towards wealth, or away from it, your reasons make up your *Personal Money Matrix.* The next Chapter is about giving a **voice** to the subconscious being that creates the *matrix,* and letting it express some things we may have been avoiding.

It's called the **Money Matrix Method.**™

CHAPTER FOUR

The Money Matrix Method™

MEDICAL DISCLAIMER: The method described in this chapter, book and on related websites is experimental in nature, and based on the author's clinical experiences. This method is *not* a medical, psychiatric, or psychological procedure, nor should it be considered as part of any medical, psychiatric, or psychological or protocol.

The practice or use the methods or techniques given herein may trigger some emotional responses that may be uncomfortable. Use them at your own risk. If you are on medication, or are under the care of a therapist or doctor, you should consult with him or her before practicing or using these methods or techniques.

The Four Phases

The concept behind the *Money Matrix Method*™ is fairly involved, and you can read about this in more depth in my book <u>The Logical Soul.</u>[R]

However in this book, rather than delving into one's subconscious mind – that which Freud defined as "a cauldron of seething excitation" – I will focus alone on certain **statements about MONEY,** and ways you can discover and change the *direct psychological links (i.e., hidden decisions) that directly affect these statements.*

The *Money Matrix Method*™ (or MMM) is very straightforward and simple. There are **4 steps** (or phases) that any decision goes through to be changed. I'll go over the first two in this book, and give some links where you can go to get more information on the last two:

1. **Prepare** the session with a partner or friend.
2. **Discover** what holds you back. Test 7 inner decisions using **muscle testing** to determine your capacity for attracting, earning and keeping wealth.
3. **Access** - Determine whether or not you have access to change these decisions. If not, *get* access, and
4. **Resolve** the conflicts by changing the inner Matrix Decisions.

Step 1: Preparation

The whole process (a "session") is designed to take about 30 minutes, but may take longer until you get the hang of it. So have a second person - a partner, a spouse, a family member, a friend - who can go through this process with you. They should also be familiar with how the method works, and willing to work with you on a regular basis.

Don't know anyone like this? Find someone you think would be receptive, give them a copy of this book, and ask if they would work with you. Or form your own Meetup group in your city or area. It is also a great way to develop lasting friendships.

The best way, however, is to locate a chiropractor, doctor or therapist who uses *The Logical Soul®* or the *Money Matrix Method™* in his or her practice. If you know someone like that, great. If not, please give them a copy of this book, or direct them to our websites to learn more about our professional training (when available).

The purpose of a "session" is to discover and define you or your partner's difficulty with money. This may at first glance appear to be simple, i.e., it's staring you in the face every day! But it often runs much deeper than that, and why it is helpful to work with someone else.

Talking with another person also adds an extra dimension to our self-knowledge. Because we tend to have ideas about ourselves and the way we're going, it's very difficult to see ourselves the way

others see us. Another person can have access to our inner motivation when we may not even realize it is there.

Sit with the other person. Whether you know this person very well or not, be sure to first have an understanding of the purpose of this session: *to find, access, and change hidden decisions about money.*

The interview is **not** about how we are doing, the weather, the news, what we are doing at work, how our life is going, or any of that stuff. It's about issues that we hardly ever talk about: our fears, anxieties, resentments and things that bog us down, or make us dull and ineffective.

If you are interviewing the other person (it could be a male or female, but for purposes of this exercise I will use the masculine pronoun), ask him

"What's your most pressing money issue today?"

Now that's a very simple question, but it has a very important component to it. By asking what is up for him *"today"* (or *"now"*) he begins to focus on how his body feels. In other words, he observes what is happening in his body or mind that is causing a concern right this minute.

Your main job, by the way, is to **listen.** Once the process begins, it's OK to take some notes. No one will talk – especially about deep-seated fears or concerns – if the person they are speaking to is yawning, looking at his watch, or glancing at the floor. This part, by the way, is the hardest thing for some people to do – saying *nothing* while another person talks.

Just notice the feeling and let it go. The *Money Matrix Method*™ happens naturally by itself, but you must get out of the way. Put your ego aside for the time allotted and simply hold the space for the other person to speak and share.

Assuming you can do this, let's proceed to the "meat" of the method . . .

The 7 Wealth Decisions

There are **seven decisions** that make up your personal Money Matrix. Each statement has to do with a particular category, such as:

1. Self-Worth
2. Acceptance
3. Earning Capacity
4. Action Commitment
5. Father
6. Mother
7. Ancestors

While these items in the list may seem strange to you, they relate to our most *intimate, hidden* or *subconscious* decisions about money.

> "Money issues" are mostly about RELATIONSHIPS to yourself and others closest to you. Even if you never knew, or rebelled against, your parents or family, they are as much a part of you as your eye color. If you want to attract more money into your life, just try on the idea for right now. Once the results come, you'll be pleasantly surprised!

You will be testing the LEVELS at which you or your partner goes "weak." A "weak" arm test indicates a "no" (more on this in the next chapter). By using this test you can determine, for example, how *MUCH* money your partner can accept.

Through testing, you determine whether or not a statement made by your partner (or you, if self-testing) is "true" or "not true." It's a powerful way to uncover your limiting decisions about wealth – one at a time!

CHAPTER FIVE

How to Determine Your #1 Limiting Wealth Factor

The SECOND STEP in the *Money Matrix Method*™ is called **Discovery.** This step is where you TEST the truth of each statement made by your partner. It is also the step where you can pin down the #1 Factor, or hidden Matrix Decision that holds you back from success.

Step 2: Discovery

Too many therapies and "prosperity consciousness" methods rely on some kind of theories or rituals that supposedly change the subconscious mind, but seldom produce real results. This can be costly. Before you spend a lot of money and time, you might want to first find out *exactly which inner decisions support your money goals,* and which ones reject them.

Discovery is the method of getting early feedback from the body to find out whether or not success is even possible! Wouldn't it be helpful to find out you even _like_ owning a restaurant, for example, before you saddle yourself with a big loan and choose the location?? If a particular path for making money doesn't feel or test strong, move on to something else. Please! Hopes and affirmations by themselves don't pay the rent!

Discovery starts at the moment of inquiry when you start to get to the "I-don't-knows" from your partner. It's the point at which **muscle testing** (or some other form of feedback) becomes crucial. The body will begin to give us answers about the "why" and the "why not" of any given statement.

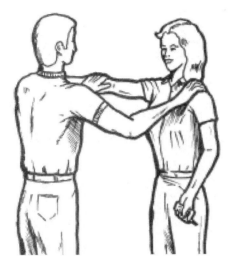

Instant feedback is also important as visible proof to show us someone inside is speaking! In our mind, when we see and feel our partner's arm muscle going weak we know we have hit on something important for him. As you will see very soon, a weak muscle indicates a **NO**, whereas a strong muscle shows a **YES.**

In our partner's mind, feeling his arm muscle going weak sends a message to his brain, both conscious and subconscious, saying:

"I'm lying to myself,"

"I'm not truthful with myself," etc.

This alone is a very powerful transforming event for most people.

If you have no partner, you can use what is called "self-testing." While this is not as ideal as using a mate or partner, it can still be pretty effective. Visit www.moneymatrixmethod.com/bonus for your free video lessons on how to do this.

While self-testing is OK, it involves more self-referral. With a partner it's a little harder to fib your way through the process. Having a partner to work with allows you the freedom to focus on the statements themselves, with less concern about whether or not you are doing it right.

How to Muscle Test

Use muscle testing with a partner, spouse or friend. Test any convenient muscle - say an arm muscle - by holding up their arm while using a few fingers to press on the arm after saying "Hold." If their arm tests strong (i.e., does not give under the pressure), that indicates a "yes" by the body. If the arm tests slightly weaker or rubbery (i.e., goes down), this may indicate a negative finding.

By the way, muscle testing is not a contest. If the muscle stays strong, don't keep pushing harder. Use 3 fingers and about 3 pounds of pressure for each statement tested. When testing, start with known **true** factors, such as your name, to see if the muscles tests strong. If your name is Larry, say "My name is Larry." If you test weak, keep testing until you get a strong signal every time. Then test something you know is **false.** If you remain strong with these statements, keep practicing until it becomes weak with each attempt.

By testing this way, you will be able to get instant feedback from the body (and subconscious mind) that either this is a **yes** or **no** ("not yes"). With the *Money Matrix Method*™, you are able to discover the overall ***congruence*** between feelings and statements or affirmations.

Again, work with a partner if at all possible. A partner can determine when a muscle is weak or strong, while during self-testing you may be tempted to block such information. While there can also be false tests with a partner, it's less likely.

If for some reason you cannot get an accurate reading using any muscle testing, you may have other factors intervening. Get my free video training at www.moneymatrixmethod.com/bonus to learn ways to overcome this. Meanwhile, you might also try switching arms when one gets tired.

During testing you'll find there are a lot of things in your life you *thought* were true that turn out to be false. You may also find out there are a lot of thoughts, feelings, ideas, dreams and affirmations that you *thought* were right on target, but turn out to be *false ideals* because your *hidden decisions were sabotaging all attempts to make them happen!* Such is the power of instant feedback.

See www.incomeathomespot.com to get a complete training course on how to learn and use every aspect of the *Money Matrix Method*™, including the 4 Steps, muscle testing, other kinds of feedback, and detailed video coaching on building an online business that can serve as your primary income, or to promote another business.

Hey, I'm Not So Sure ...

You might have questions at this point, such as:

> *"Well, how do I know you're not pushing harder?"*

> *"How do I know this really works?"*

> *"Why should I trust this?"* or

> *"Is this accurate?"*

Fair questions. But have you stopped to consider that, although this test is not perfect, **a)** it's a cheap and accessible lie-detector test, and **b)** I told you I wasn't going into a lot of explanations. If you want more information, please refer to my blog at www.logicalsoul.com, or to my first book The Logical Soul®.

Muscle testing works. If you would prefer to have more accuracy, feel free to invest in a polygraph machine, or Computerized Voice Stress Analyzer, or CVSA. They will give more accuracy, but at a high cost.

The Seven Test Statements

When you are prepared to test the person, have him repeat (out loud) the following ***Money Statements*** while your test the muscle. The write down the first dollar amount for each statement that makes him weak:

1. *"I'm worth at least* [a certain amount of money]."

2. *"I can easily accept* [a certain amount of money]."

3. *"I can easily earn* [a certain amount of money]."

4. *"I am committed to take action on* [a certain amount of money]."

5. Test the first 4 statements, adding *"in the presence of my father."*

6. Test the first 4 statements, adding *"in the presence of my mother."*

7. Test the first 4 statements, adding *"in the presence of my ancestors."*

Again, you are testing for the LEVELS of each statement. Once known, these statements are called *Hidden Matrix Decisions*, since they reflect one's inner reality about money. The **_lowest value_** of all these tests will determine your #1 most limiting wealth factor . . .

Starting on the next page, I cover these concepts in more details.

1. Worth

How much are you worth?

Believe it or not, you have a number inside that matches what you think you're worth. Test your partner to find out the amount of money that makes him go weak. Then write that dollar amount down.

"But Michael," you may protest, *"aren't human beings priceless?!"*

Yes and no. While I agree that you cannot put a dollar figure on the lives of human beings, the number is still there. Remember, you are dealing with <u>*subconscious yearnings and directives,*</u> where a different logic is in effect. Don't try to rationalize subconscious decisions. All you end up doing is shutting down this valuable communication with your inner being.

2. Accept

How much money can you accept?

I like to preface this by saying, "My best friends, Donald Trump, Bill Gates, and Warren Buffet have all shaved their heads, retired to a Buddhist monastery, and given up all their material wealth. Before they left, they pooled all their assets together, and gave me their checkbook along with orders that I must *give it all away within 24 hours*. Time is almost up, so *how much money can I write you a check for right now*?!"

Test, and write down the lowest number that makes your partner go weak.

3. Easily Earn

How much money can you easily earn?

This value has to do with earning *capacity,* not actual current earnings. If your partner is a self-employed entrepreneur, this would have to do with how much he or she thinks they could conceivably earn in a month or year.

If your partner has a job, this number would be in addition to his or her salary. This number might also consider earnings potential from any side business, investment, inheritance, or any other wealth-building sources.

Test, and write down the lowest number that makes your partner go weak.

4. Commitment to Action

This value has to do with direct action based on a clear *path* and clear *commitment.* While *Accepting* is allowing money to come to you, *taking action* means *going out and getting the money*! It also means taking whatever legal, moral and ethical steps possible to secure this money.

Before testing this statement, have your partner describe the action he or she is committed to taking.

You might then test several alternatives and choose the strongest one.

Again, test and write down the lowest number that makes your partner go weak.

5. Father Issues

The presence of the **father** is an archetype for the family's connection with the outside world of structure, work and business. This influence, therefore, is practically all-pervasive for most when it comes to money. It is also either a powerful motivator, or powerful deterrent to making money.

Whether or not the father and mother are still alive, doesn't matter. The main thing is that your partner knows what their presence means. By invoking it along with the first 4 money statements, you are able to touch a deep connection that may invoke a powerful response.

Test, and write down the lowest number that makes your partner go weak for each of the first 4 statements when used with the additional phrase *"in the presence of my father."*

6. Mother Issues

The presence of the mother is obviously archetypal, and provides our motivation (or deterrent) to create, manifest, and take care of our prospects, clients and customers.

Test, and write down the lowest number that makes your partner go weak for each of the first four (4) statements when used with the additional phrase *"in the presence of my mother."*

7. Ancestral Influences

We ARE our ancestors! Consequently, their influence is felt by us, even if we never knew them! I could write an entire book on this, but again, I promised to keep this one brief and to the point.

I must point out, however, that early work by French biologist **Jean-Philippe Lamark** in the early 1800's paved the way for us to consider certain behaviors as hereditary. Also, the in-depth research on *family constellations* by contemporary German psychologist **Bert Hellinger** has provided confirmation that MMM and *The Logical Soul®* techniques are on target.

When testing, write down the lowest number that makes your partner go weak for each of the first 4 statements when used with the additional phrase *"in the presence of my ancestors."* If you get mixed signals, you might narrow this testing down to one branch of ancestors, e.g., your father's side.

In Conclusion . . .

If you want to know your #1 Limiting Wealth Factor, use the muscle testing to find out instantly. Through muscle testing we can actually map out our *hidden Matrix Decisions.* You can measure where you stand with money so you know what you need to address. Simple.

You set the levels. Once you learn the whole *Money Matrix Method™*, you can repeat the process until you reach higher and higher levels and feel comfortable owning, accepting, earning and acting on some new-found wealth. When the affirmation becomes true for you, i.e., you feel it inside and your body is saying "yes," you can go as high as you want!

By the way, these statements are never true on an absolute sense because there's no such thing as "absolute truth" according to modern science. What we are discovering in this step, actually, is *whether or not something is **true for you** or **not true for you** (or your partner)*. That's all.

Regardless of the answer, however, it's going to save you a lot of time, a lot of money, and a lot of heartaches, headaches, efforts and frustrations later on. Wouldn't you think it is wise to know these numbers before, say, investing your life savings into a fast food franchise??

So the "truth" about you and money is that through muscle testing you can determine your hidden capacity for attracting, earning, accepting, and keeping money or wealth.

In the next chapter I'll go over ways to access and change most of these decisions.

CHAPTER SIX

How to Have Massive Success!

The third and fourth steps of the *Money Matrix Method*™ are a bit more involved, and beyond the scope of this book. They are called **Access** and **Resolution,** and I offer a training course to show you how to use Access to change 100% of your wealth issues.

Meanwhile, I can show you how to affect changes for 75-80% of the limiting beliefs, decisions or factors that keep you stuck in the *No-Wealth Zone* of the matrix.

Hidden Decisions

The "No-Wealth Zone" is populated by things we simply don't want to remember. If the pain becomes too great, our subconscious mind will oblige us and blot it from our memory. A big loss is one example. Divorce is another. Serious pain from a disease or accident is often one. There are also memories from attacks, abuse, rapes, miscarriages, or other serious intrusions that affect our lives, sanity and well-being.

There are many reasons we block out memories. One of the biggest reasons is because of **shame -** either yours, or that which you inherited from your family or ancestors. Once in place, shame is often disassociated while we enlist the more "acceptable" emotions and tactics (like fear, anger, blame or justification) to keep it all hidden.

In just about every case where loss of power or happiness is evident, shame is a factor. Even when the fault is clearly not ours, there is a natural aversion to revealing our hidden secrets, fears, phobias, and lack of knowledge to others who (we believe) may use this against us.

The root of this goes back many generations and perhaps millions of years. You have inherited a certain amount of animal and tribal behavior that manifests itself in the Limbic System of your brain. The thoughts and decisions emanating from this area are very competitive and survival-oriented, and often lead to uncontrollable desires, impulses, and behaviors, like addiction.

This is the reason why so much corruption exists in group dynamics such as politics and business. *This may also be the reason why you are not attracting more money into your life!*

Step 3: Access

Access is really the *heart* of both the *Money Matrix Method*™ and the *Logical Soul*®. It is what makes these techniques different than other self-improvement and goal-setting techniques and other therapies out there.

Most traditional therapies assume two things:

1. The patient can change if only he or she *wants* to change, and
2. It takes a fairly long time to get the desired results.

The *Logical Soul®* and *Money Matrix Method*™ expose these assumptions for what they are: outdated. There IS a better – and faster – way!

The first assumption - that you can change if you want to - is a myth. Without ACCESS to the deeper hidden decisions that run your life, you can "want" to change forever, but real change will not come except by accident, years of massaging your feelings, or by grace.

Even if you wanted to change – and hired a pro to help you - "talk therapy," according to a recent *New York Times* article on psychotherapy, "is dead." And this was traditionally how psychotherapists earned their keep, i.e., spending the years necessary to "bring out" the patient. But no more. Talk takes time. Psycho-tropic drugs don't, so the doctor spends less time and makes more money.

The second assumption is that it takes a long time to get results. This is actually true . . . *using the older methods of therapy!* With *the Logical Soul®* and *MMM,* however, results are measured based on the decisions accessed and changed. The deeper the decision, the more powerful the results.

The Logical Soul® / MMM - for the most part - provide access to changing deep-rooted decisions without churning up all your volatile emotions and fears. These techniques are like using a scalpel to cut to the heart of the hidden decision, *NOT* massaging around the edges in hopes that change will happen. As a consequence, the connection between the hidden decision and results is made without having to slug through lifetimes of "stuff."

Another way to understand Access is to see it as a way of getting beyond what I call **"The Wall"** - that thing you hit when you can't go any deeper inside. Every other technique I've ever seen or used has run up against – been confounded by - this wall. It's that subconscious barrier that stops us from getting the answers we really seek.

You see, when you set goals, most of the effort goes into fighting and trying to get beyond this "Wall." The *Money Matrix Method*™ is designed to DISSOLVE the Wall by making it your *friend*! Consequently, MUCH less effort is used to fight the Wall, and much more results can be realized!

The *mortar* that holds this Wall together is *your personal story* . . .

Your Personal Story

Your **personal story** is your reason for being. It tells you what is true and what is false. What is glorious and what is hogwash. It keeps you safe, and tells you what is OK and what is not.

Your personal story is made up of what are called *"Meme Clusters"* – or thoughts that propagate themselves in our minds over and over again – that give us our self-image, or quest. But it's not so important to understand that now; I will touch on this later. The main thing to know here is that your personal story has been *your greatest single tool for survival* in this world . . . . and *it's also based primarily on lies!*

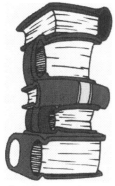

For the most part, *your personal story is a collection of beliefs and ideas rooted in decisions you made up about reality a long time ago.* The problems only come in when what you *think* is the truth is actually just your *story* about what you experienced.

And most people have this. Let's face it, when it comes to a choice between the truth and our story, we choose the story. Why? Because it's *OUR truth, dammit!*

So, in this way you keep your personal story in place. There is also not much room for change. There's not much room to grow. Only those decisions that fit into the neat little cubbyholes you've built for yourself are welcome.

All the other things fall to the wayside. If you have difficulty attracting money and repeat affirmations like "I am attracting millions into my life," "I am a money magnet," or whatever, the truth of these statements won't hold up. *Your personal story will not accept these affirmations or statements.* They are simply not heard! This is why your arm goes weak in testing.

How to Test Access

After you have determined that your partner goes weak with certain levels of income, worth, etc., the NEXT step is to find out if he has *ACCESS* to change these *hidden Matrix Decisions.*

Ask your partner (or yourself) to say out loud:

> **"Access is available to change this program."**

If that tests **strong,** then proceed to the next step.

If that tests **weak,** there is a process for getting access, but it is too involved to go into here, since it will require extra training or private sessions. For the majority of statements, however, access IS available, so let's go on that assumption for now.

Ask your partner to say:

> **"I allow (partner's name) access to change this program."**

You are asking the "subconscious being" to verify that the "conscious being" (indicated by the partner's name) has conscious access. If the answer to THIS statement is **strong,** then you know it is fairly easy to change the underlying Matrix Decision. Go on to the next section.

If the answer to THIS statement is **weak,** however, you will need to get further training. Check out your options at www.moneymatrixmethod.com/training.

Assuming You Have Conscious Access

Visit www.moneymatrixmethod.com/bonus where I will show you how to get access to the other side of most hidden decisions. This is the *real key* to *The Money Matrix Method*™, and the whole process takes about 10-15 minutes.

You can learn this powerful process and *change your life in minutes, not years.* You can get beyond "the Wall" and change what I call hidden or **archetypal Matrix decisions,** these key decisions at the very core of your essence, those "lynchpin decisions" that govern who you are, and what the world is around you.

By changing these decisions, you unlock the <u>secret of your own wealth mastery.</u> THEN (and only then) can you make sense of all the success, motivational, and goal-setting courses you've been collecting!

> **DISCLAIMER:** *I repeat – I am not a psychologist or psychiatrist, although I have done extensive counseling. Money Matrix Method*™ *is safe and effective as prescribed, but <u>don't deviate from the method as outlined</u>. Experimenting with this procedure may be harmless, or it could cause emotional or mental upset. When I first started using this process back in 1992, the releases often took days. It now takes only minutes – when I stick to what works.*

The Access Process

"Getting access," in a nutshell, means asking your (or your partner's) inner child (or parent or ancestor) for access. You're asking the one who first made the Matrix decision. <u>*Only the one who made the decision can change the decision.*</u> The person himself, his inner child, parent or ancestor is the only who can do this.

It goes something like this: Ask your partner to close his eyes and focus on the last statement that made him go weak. How does it feel? Where in the body does he have a sensation, if there is one.

If there is a sensation in the head, heart, abdomen or elsewhere, tell him to focus and describe it to you. Then say:

> *"Go back to the very first time you remember . . . maybe not the first time, but the first time you remember feeling this* [sensation] *. . . and let me know when you're there. "*
>
> After he responds, ask more questions to get a clearer picture of the story, e.g., "How old are you?" "What's happening?" "What decision about money did you make at that point...?"
>
> At this point, I usually have the adult rescue he child and take him or her to a safe place, then to where I call *"the place of decision"* that is part of the **Resolution** Process . . .

If there is NO sensation, or no memories come up, I just usually assume that the decision was programmed into the child at an early age – often by a parent or ancestor. When this is the case, I request a visualized conference with the child, myself and ancestor (or parent) in order to request the elder's permission to "let go of the promise to carry this burden."

IMPORTANT NOTE: To get complete access, you must **establish trust** with the inner child. You do this by asking the child to bring in someone he trusts already – a guide or trusted being, religious figure, pet or ancestor. Use this to get access to hidden decisions, to change them and change your life dramatically in minutes.

Step 4: Resolution

I have created a guided visualization to the Resolution Step called *"the place of decision"* that you can download free and use for this step at www.moneymatrixmethod.com/bonus.

The main thing to consider during the Resolution Phase is to *integrate the new decision into the body and nervous system.* This process allows for both a conscious and subconscious integration to take place. Without this, all you have is wishful thinking.

Up until now, I've been discussing how to overcome individual hidden decisions by accessing and changing them. In the next chapter, I will open the door to a radical new theory and method for changing whole patterns of hidden decisions at once.

The discovery of this theory and method is brand new to MMM, and was added just before the book went to the publisher. So enjoy . . . and USE it!

A Word about Forgiveness

In the Bonus section you will also find a video on the **"Logical Soul Forgiveness Process"** or LSFP. I included this because it's been my experience in working with thousands of people over the past 30 years that built-up resentment is one of the strongest ways to STOP your growing success in all areas.

Your potential customers can sense anger and resentment a mile away . . . and will probably avoid you like the plague.

Even if all the other factors in your matrix test strong, you might still be pushing others (and money) away. Muscle test to determine if you forgive others – particularly in your family or those close to you, like a spouse.

Forgiveness is a powerful thing, but LSFP is much more different than anything you've probably ever tried before. Use it, and great things can come to you!

CHAPTER SEVEN

The Great Escape: Getting Beyond Your Mind Viruses

Your *personal story* is made up of multiple **"Mind Viruses"** that were originally created to help you survive, but now act as potent barriers to your success.

What is a Mind Virus?

A mind virus has a scientific name: **Meme.** The term was first used by Oxford Biologist **Richard Dawkins** in 1976, and popularized by **Richard Brodie** in his book *Virus of the Mind (Integral Press, 1996).*

According to Wikipedia, a **meme** is a unit of social information. It is a relatively newly coined term and identifies ideas or beliefs that are transmitted from one person or group of people to another. The concept comes from an analogy: as *genes* transmit biological information, *memes* can be said to transmit idea and belief information. The study of *memetics* arose in the 1990's to explore the behavior of memes.

The reason a meme is considered a "virus" is because its primary motivation is *its own survival and propagation.* Nothing else matters… at least to the meme!

A simple example of a meme is the song that keeps running over and over in your head. Trying to kick it out does not good . . . it just wants to keep propagating itself! Other meme examples might include socially-mandated beliefs that are designed to control behavior and response; beliefs like

> *"Save the children"*
> *"You can't always get what you want."*
> *"Money is the root of all evil"* . . . etc.

Other memes form the basis of cults, family stories, religion and politics. Some – like the Catholic Church – grow and prosper, while others – consider the Luddites – eventually die out due to irrelevance. Like their cousins – genes - memes are destined to either wither on the vine, or beat out competing memes for dominance. This is where the real battle for survival of the fittest takes place – *in your mind!*

Brodie points out there are both helpful and harmful memes, just as there are good and bad viruses. A meme, in and of itself, is not a bad thing. It just needs to be recognized for what it is, and either embraced or discarded as the need arises.

If a meme is positive, you may want to keep it, or even cultivate it. Scripture such as *"These things I have, ye shall have also; and even greater things"* is a very helpful meme" for cultivating wealth, whereas distorted scriptural phrases like *"Money is the root of all evil"* does nothing to help you pay the bills! You must choose which memes serve your needs and goals . . . and which ones don't.

The Origin of Memes

Memes arose as a way of forming relationships to survive - mankind's most powerful motivation. Because of their fears, ancient man banded together to form **tribes,** or small groups who hunted together, mated, and helped each other.

As a member of the tribe you were afforded certain protections from wild animals, invaders, and the vagaries of nature. You had much-needed help to survive. If you were brave, strong and cunning, you could even rise to a position of power.

But tribal membership also came with a downside. You had to obey the laws of the tribe . . . and sometimes these laws were severe and malicious. You usually had laws for everything: eating, mating, property, and just about every mode of behavior or human activity. These laws were designed for one purpose only, **i.e., the survival of the tribe.** The idea was that if you kept surprises to a minimum, there would be less danger.

The tribe's rules, laws and dogmas were usually strictly enforced, and handed down from one generation to another. This habit of handing ideas and rules down became the memes that formed the basis of our **traditions, myths** and **legends.** Oral traditions and archetypal stories are good examples of helpful memes that were passed down for generations.

In evolutionary terms, it is relatively easy to take a set of memes, codify them, and create a lasting set of beliefs called "laws" to keep handing down to each succeeding generation. But here's the rub . . .

The meme is a mind virus and you, as a human being, are merely a *"carrier."* The meme is an intelligence that is independent of human thought or will, but uses these and other human qualities to propagate itself.

Meme Clusters

A **Meme Cluster** is a tightly-bound set of memes that serve as a "story" or a complete narrative. This story is a kind of "society for memes." Just as genes band together to form algae and humans, memes congregate to form a *mental/emotional parasite* – a powerful intelligence created through millions of years of evolution that has insidiously taken over your life!!

Yes, you are host to parasites in your own mind . . . hidden in plain sight! Religions and political organizations are examples of meme clusters, but certainly not the only ones. You are also ruled by memes that govern your relationship to food, sex, love, work, money, happiness and health.

Mental parasites, just like their physical brethren, are able to set up shop and thrive for two reasons:
  a) We feed them constantly, and
  b) We don't know they exist!

Depending on how caught up you are with the world, you are most likely carrying hundreds of meme clusters without any awareness of doing so. In fact, you may consider your Meme Clusters as part of *your own self*, i.e., the *I, me,* or *mine.*

"I just can't get ahead" may be one example of a meme having to do with victimhood, struggle, lack, and suffering.   But this statement is just the tip of the Meme Cluster iceberg, where 99% of the cluster remains hidden.

Other – unspoken – memes no doubt make up the cluster. These may include hidden decisions like:
   "Life is a struggle,"
   "Daddy never liked me,"
   "Something bad always happens,"
   "I will always be this way,"
   "Having money will push away my friends and family,"
   "I'm too tired". . . ad infinitum.

The hidden parts of the cluster keep reinforcing all the others.   And, like the tribe defending its own members, the cluster itself will come to the defense of one of its members if it is threatened with extinction. In one recent session, I tested over *493 different memes in one cluster,* and we are usually host to hundreds of clusters!!

Where They Come From

Memes and Meme Clusters come from so many sources, it's hard to list them all. Here are a few of the more obvious sources:

Parental (and ancestral) influences. This is your fundamental source of the deepest negativity. Beliefs handed down faithfully over many generations tend to continue being handed down. The methods in this book can help defuse many of these, although it may take a while if your family or ancestral tree was particularly dysfunctional.

The Media. If you watch the news or listen to talk radio, you are no doubt aware that these "festering meme pools" fill you mind and heart with stuff you simply don't need! While the latest on the New York serial killer may be interesting, the affect it has on your psyche – and your wallet - is devastating.

Turn off the TV and radio, and stop reading the newspaper (except for sports and funnies). You won't miss anything, I promise you. If you are worried about not being informed, don't. Truly relevant news has a way of finding you. People will talk. If you addiction is really bad and you MUST have a news fix, sign up for one weekly news magazine, or go to the local library once a week.

The same goes for music. Heavy metal music, for example, will totally jar your nervous system. If you don't like classical or easy listening music, carry around motivational CDs instead.

Negative people. I have made quite an interesting observation, and that is that negative people DON'T "make" you negative, *they only bring out the negativity you've been denying in yourself!* If you feel negative after hanging out with Miserable Molly, it may be because you already had the seed of negativity within yourself.

<u>Do this</u>: work on your own "stuff" or hidden decisions and meme attachments. Eventually you will find – like I did – that negative people no longer bother you. In fact, they usually *avoid* you!

For example, I used to hang around negative people out of a sense of obligation or loyalty. Now I don't. Negative people have pretty much disappeared from my life.

If I find myself in negative company, however, I understand quite well the pain these people are feeling inside, but choose not to take it on myself. This way I can be both compassionate AND stay happy! If you are feeling anger about being around angry people, guess what? You are still taking on their stuff!

E-mail.   If you don't pass on the "blessings of the Madonna" you will NOT die or lose a fortune. Trust me; I know.   Delete negative and time-wasting emails, rss feeds, texts, and social media posts – as well as the people who send them - from your life and you will smile more often.

<u>Do this</u>: Check posts and emails twice a day for 10 minutes each time. More than that and you will never find true success. Most are pure memes!

How to *REALLY* Change Your Life...

While you will never be able to clear you mind and life of all memes, meme clusters, and problems, you can eventually let go of the *attachment* to them. Once this happens, I call it "awakening."

"Awakening" or "enlightenment" are terms we normally associate with spiritual matters . . . a type of human awareness that transcends memes. This may be so, but that's a subject too vast to cover in any one book, if it can be covered at all.

If there is a way to transform *Meme Cluster Consciousness* to *Awakening,* it might involve these three steps:

1. *Becoming aware of your clusters* as they arise,
2. *Discovering the "Lynchpin Decisions"* that bind you to the clusters, and
3. *Stepping into a different Story* or Archetype.

A "lynchpin decision" is any hidden decision that is the central prime directive for a group of other hidden decisions, memes, or meme clusters. You can change a "lynchpin decision" the same way you can a "regular" hidden decision, but the change is a bit more radical. For one thing, it could change your whole perception of what is "real."

Just like in the movie *"The Matrix,"* there is a level of reality where you may not feel comfortable after taking the "red pill" by changing deeply-rooted lynchpin decisions!

If, however, you are TRULY READY to step into wealth from the inside-out (and if you currently live in the 'no-wealth zone') you have to be willing to take on a new and different PERSONAL STORY or **"Archetype"** with radically different meme clusters!

NOTE: If you are like some people, changing your basic archetype may be too much too fast. I understand. You should then work on smaller stuff – individual matrix decisions - until you feel ready to move more quickly.

So what NEW personal story (Archetype) can you take on? The Father figure? The Madonna? Priest? Trickster? Lover? Villain? All of these characters are essential to every culture, and one of them may be the key to your success! But you won't know WHICH one until you've cleared your head enough to grasp it!

Your new set of memes, i.e., your archetypal character, is ageless and deathless. "You" may come and go, but your *archetype will live forever.* This, incidentally, is *the key to your legacy,* or what you hand down to succeeding generations.

"But how" you may ask "does this have anything to do with money and success, and why should I care?" Here's the answer:

An ***Archetype*** is an Internal Force
that moves and motivates you either
towards money and success . . .
or *away* from it.

Your **personal archetype** is the foundation of your purpose, i.e., your reason for being. You may or may not know what it is but it's still there, waiting to express itself either as a constructive - or *destructive* – force in your life! It's the WHY in your life, the reason you wake up in the morning and the reason that keeps you alive and thinking.

Shakespeare revealed his knowledge of archetypes when he wrote *"All the world's a stage, and the men and women merely players."* He understood <u>we are part of something larger than ourselves</u>, and that the role we play in this is already assigned to us!

The *only question* you have to ask yourself is this: "am I playing my role CONSCIOUSLY and WILLINGLY, or am I choosing to remain unconscious, driven by forces beyond my understanding?"

Let's assume you choose to be conscious; that's why you're reading this book! OK, then, what's next?

Understanding the *"Wealth Archetypes"*

CHAPTER EIGHT

How to Discover Your *REAL* Motivation

The Evolution of Wealth

Historically, the idea of wealth originated in the **Zero Sum game.** For thousands of years, mankind has fought one another over territory, resources and religion. The prevailing belief during this time? "If you win, I lose," and vice-versa. You steal my woman; I kill you. If I need your land, you must die. This was the most prevalent Meme Cluster.

The only exception to this rule came when groups of people, feeling more threatened by their environment than their neighbor, decided to come together and form a mutually-protective bond. These social bonds – tribes, and nations – were initially founded on the need for mutual survival, but eventually evolved into expressions of love, relationship, and community.

Tribal and nation rules were put in place to *avoid* competition for resources within the tribe itself. If you crossed this line, you were disciplined. If you stole from others in the group, you were locked up, ostracized or killed. Those in the tribe quickly learned that **cooperation** – rather than competition

– got the most results with the minimum of effort and risk.

While there have been obvious exceptions - nations ruled by tyrants, warlords or dictators - our communal need to survive eventually gave rise to the idea of cooperation, or **Win-Win.** You win some, I also have enough.

> ➢ **In a Zero-Sum Game,** there is only one "pie." Each person can only be allotted portions of this pie, or we must all fight one another to get "our fair share" of the pie. Resources are limited.

> ➢ **In a Win-Win Game,** we simply work together to make the pie bigger! A bigger pie means more resources. This in turn means less fighting and more cooperation. Resources are UN-limited!

The Win-Win Game, however, *requires a shift in consciousness*, i.e., some degree of awakening. If you play this game, you must arrive at the point where you can truly be OK with others having more *and NOT automatically fall into fear, denial, anger or numbness.* These emotions – programmed into us through millions of years of evolution – are what keep us small.

And broke.

Very Good Reasons To Stay Broke

If you are poor, broke . . . or simply lack the money and resources you want and need, why is that? What does it feel like?

Take a few minutes. Put down the book and make a note of how this idea of being broke actually feels. Then look inside and see what feeds this feeling, or meme cluster. If you are honest with yourself, you may come face to face with one of the biggest archetypes that blocks people – **the Victim.**

If you are running the victim meme cluster, you are knee-deep in a Zero Sum Game . . . and *losing!* If so, look to see which personal story you have also created *in order to justify losing.*

Based on the fact that your **personal archetype** (or personal story) supports the assorted *hidden decisions* you have about money, all the thoughts and feelings you have will support this story, i.e., *the meme cluster of reasons why you should stay broke!*

If, for example, you are broke because of losses in the stock market, the economy is bad, etc., look to *why* these particular reasons are important. For one thing, most of it is out of your hands, right? Therefore you cannot be responsible.

It is easy in this situation to blame outside forces for your financial condition, but the truth is, *you made the decision* to be in the stock market, invest in real estate, and take a risk in business or investments.

Accepting the fact that there are NO guarantees in life is hard, but it's the truth.

By exercising "victim thoughts" you reinforce the personal story, and also perpetuate the victim meme cluster. This, in turn, leads to MORE opportunities to be a victim. When some "can't miss" opportunity comes along, you'll be on that bandwagon too. Then predictably you'll soon be broke again. And since the meme *"misery loves company"* is also a part of this cluster, you will begin to "spread the gospel" to others!

The Victim, however, is not the only story arising from the eternal fountain of financial misery. It's only the most widespread.

Below are a few examples of how your self-image directly affects your relationship to money (or lack of it). See if any of them ring true for you:

1. **I am the Warrior-Monk.** I fight for causes and against the greedy oppressors. Power corrupts and I seek to remain un-corrupted.

2. **I am the Hero.** I have no need of anything except the thanks from those for whom I sacrifice. My mission is to save the planet. Money is useful, so I'm constantly seeking donations from those who have it so that I might continue my important work.

3. **I am the Madonna/Savior.** I am above the desire to have money and riches. Blessed are the poor...

4. **I am the Child/Innocent.** I don't know what to do or how to get or attract money. I do affirmations hoping it will show up.

5. **I am the Lover.** Who's got time to make money when my gift is my love, and nurturing my love is all there is!

6. **I am the Shaman.** I will manifest money though my deep understanding of universal forces. Only when I'm ready...

7. **I am the Rebel.** I have no need or desire for money. It is the root of all evil and the tool of the oppressor, i.e., "The Man." I will forever fight any and all attempts to take my freedom!

These are just some examples of how self-image impacts our ability to attract money and wealth. Essentially, however, it boils down to a single, unique idea or concept that I'll cover in the next section.

The *REAL* Reason to Stay Broke

You know what? There IS NO good reason to want more money or wealth beyond survival. If survival is all you want – and you have it – that's great! Animals do quite well without the green stuff, and of course *"the lilies of the field neither toil nor sweat..!"*

No matter what your personal story or Quest, however, it all boils down to a single concept that is so simple, you missed it in all the Wealth Seminars and Get Rich Symposia you've attended over the last umpteen years.

This concept has nothing to do with positive thinking, programming the subconscious mind, affirmations, or any of the other worn out techniques you've heard before. Ready? Here it is . . .

You are broke simply because of one thing . . .

You are a Spiritual Being NOT Wanting to Put Your Boots on the Ground!

Simple, huh? But don't get me wrong – I have nothing against a desire to be spiritual, a lover, a warrior, or a shaman. What is muddying up your financial bottom line is simply the belief you have that "I can't be on my Quest (spiritual) *and wealthy at the same time!"*

This is what I call a "linked decision," i.e., one statement or belief is linked to the other in such a way that it becomes part of your personal story. This, in turn, *will forever block you from attracting money!*

Try this: Do a simple muscle test while making the following statements,

"I choose to be here
– in the body, on the planet."

and

"I can be spiritual
and have money at the same time."

If you test weak on one or both of those
statements, you are
      a) not completely in the body and
      b) not nearly as wealthy as you want to be.

Surprised you're not in the body? Don't be. Believe
it or not, you have already done quite a LOT even if
not fully here! You made it *THIS* far didn't you?!

The ones who are completely **grounded** are the
ones who make the world <u>work</u>. Have you ever
noticed that these people are usually our leaders,
motivational speakers, manufacturers and, yes, the
wealthiest among us?

It's true. Your archetypal was born in the ozone,
lives there, and must justify continuing to stay there.
This created your current financial condition. Like it
or not, you are a space cadet looking for the big (and
wealthy) Mother Ship – and *it's not there!*

But here is the truth . . .

You can *still* be spiritual AND take decisive action towards wealth and money!

You still want wealth? Great. Here's what you must
do:

1. *Come back* in your body,
2. *Stay* in your body no matter what,
3. *Convert your story into goals* that have tangible results, and
4. *Take decisive action* towards these goals.
5. *Commit* to FINISHING these actions!

There has got to be, however, a *VERY GOOD REASON* beyond your personal story to want more money or wealth. Merely wanting is NOT enough! You've got to want MONEY as much as you want food, sex, or air to breathe! This is where self-knowledge on a deep level becomes critical.

You can't *CREATE* motivation.
You can only *DISCOVER* it!

Procrastination

Procrastination is NOT a failure of inner willpower or motivation. It is simply the subconscious assertion that something remains undone that is deemed (by the subconscious) to be more important than the action you want to take.

Use the *Money Matrix Method*™ to access and change the underlying decisions that stop you, and action becomes effortless.

Henry David Thoreau once said, "Don't stop building your castles in the air. That's where they SHOULD be! Just build the foundations under them!"

That Mother Ship needs you to get busy!

86

CHAPTER NINE

How to Discover Your Passion

True Passion Involves Win-Win

For thousands of years, mankind's only real **passion** was to **survive.** The few individuals of history who could afford to explore their life passions beyond survival were folks like kings, nobles, government leaders, church leaders, and other landed gentry.

In those days, the *Zero-Sum* game was the only game known to the "civilized" world. Attitudes of the rich were paternalistic at best, and downright nasty at their worst. The rich people had property, while the slaves and servants who attended their everyday needs had little or nothing.

The wealthy were either simply too good and too resourceful to lose, or were born into families who got that way on the backs and resources of others. Wealth in those days was usually earned through conquest, inheritance, and by supplying the needs of their tribesmen or countrymen from the toil and resources of those they conquered or exploited. Information and social status were both hard to come by, and the rich used these advantages to further enhance their estates.

Today, there are opportunities that exist beyond the wildest imaginings of even a Benjamin Franklin, Thomas Jefferson, Thomas Edison, Teddy Roosevelt, Cornelius Vanderbilt or Henry Ford. Although jobs are suddenly at a premium, the Internet has leveled the playing field and made products and services available and affordable to almost everyone.

Today, discovering your passion is both *necessary AND achievable!* Knowing your passion is *necessary* because simply aiming to <u>survive</u> will no longer suffice as a workable wealth strategy. We must learn to embrace Win-Win, if for no other reason than there are fewer and fewer peoples and resources to exploit. We simply cannot afford to kill each other anymore to get what we want! True passion demands that we *embrace*, rather than exclude.

Embracing is also necessary because – unless we accept both technology and other people – we will be left woefully behind. The tremendous influx of communication and information technologies and social media venues has leveled the playing field, but also caused a lot of internal strife in those who cannot embrace these changes.

The good news is this: your wealth is no longer limited by rulers and potentates. If you live in the west, you are not bound by family name, caste, guild, or social status. Now, you are encouraged to do your share to make the economic pie bigger. As a result of your contribution, the pie gets *really big,* as does your share of it! Small and fleet businesses can now more easily trump the big slow ones by using VERY targeted marketing to bring goods and services directly to the ideal customer.

Suddenly, both information AND social status are available to anyone with an online connection and the willingness to get it. Google brings us any information we want, and marketing and social networking can build our "list" and supply all the social status we crave.

All the treasure formerly denied us is suddenly laid at our feet. And you know what? Most people have NO CLUE what to do with it all!! They are suddenly OVERWHELMED!

The reason for this is that most people are still living in **survival** mode, and don't know how to dig out of it. Here's a way . . .

We Have Found the Enemy . . . and He is *US!*

Survival. It's a zero-sum game.

Remember Maslows' *Hierarchy of Needs* from Chapter Two? It explains a lot. But it doesn't really tell us how to get OUT of survival, only that we've got to take care of the basics before we can move upwards in the pyramid.

This book is designed to help you do just that. If you can truly increase your wealth *CAPACITY* using the *Money Matrix Method™*, you can start to open your heart and mind to some possibilities that have been lying dormant for most of your life. It's worth a try, yes?

Sometimes, finding your true PASSION only requires you take one step. *Take that step in the direction of fulfilling your most basic needs.* Right now. If you can't pay the rent, get some assistance. If you have family problems, address them head on. If you can't accomplish anything worthwhile, clean up your room or office so you can think clearer!

Whatever you do, come back into the body and accept that you are a *spiritual being learning how to be human!* Earth is imperfect, and definitely messier than Heaven, but that's just the way it is...

Do whatever it takes to clear up your "messes" as my mentor Raymond Aaron describes them. If your office is a mess of clutter, for example, set an "outrageous" goal to clean it up.

But DON'T just set one goal to clean, set **THREE.** If your *outrageous goal* is to have *a completely clean office with everything in its own file,* you know from past experience you probably won't do this. Therefore set this as your *OUTRAGEOUS GOAL.* But set two others *a bit less ideal,* so you can still feel good about yourself even if you don't accomplish everything you think is perfect.

Here's how it might look:

- **MINIMUM GOAL:** Clear off my desk into a single pile
- **TARGET GOAL:** Go through the pile and sort into related piles.
- **OUTRAGEOUS GOAL:** File away each separate pile into its own easy-to-access filing cabinet, shelf or drawer.

Raymond has a whole program he calls the **Monthly Mentor Program** dedicated to setting goals like this, in all the major areas of life (check out his whole program at www.monthlymentorreview.com). Although I've tried setting goals for many decades, Raymond's is the *ONLY* way I've been able to set – and achieve – my goals with tangible results!

Double Your Income

Make this your first money goal. I know, it sounds a bit capricious, but stick with me on this . . .

By working on your money issues with the method outlined in this book, *then* setting a goal to *double your income,* you give your subconscious mind a clear path to follow. Letting go of the old stuff is great, but unless you immediately fill it with a clear direction, you will return to your old ways simply by force of habit!

The goal to double your income, by the way, has no time period attached to it. It's a goal that allows you – without pressure – to start gathering the resources you need to eventually get there. Soon enough you will be setting clear, time-related actions goals. But for now, just be clear about your direction.

Also, doubling your income has no meaning if you currently have no income. In such a case, set the goal to have *some income or cash flow* you can feel comfortable with. If you have a job with no room for advancement, set a goal to make the same money doing something on the side – your own home business or website.

I'll go over the steps and resources you'll need to double your income in the next two chapters. Meanwhile, it's important for you to know HOW you want to get there. *First* learn to *do what you love!*

Do What You Love

Raymond Aaron also has a process of finding out what you love very quickly. He calls it his *"Love Letters"* and it goes, essentially, like this: Give yourself a set time – say 10 Minutes. Then have someone ask you in a rapid-fire manner "What do you love? What do you love? . . . "

Then you start writing. Put down everything you love on a list within the time allowed, but leave room in the margins. After you're done, put a letter next to each item that indicates its importance: H, M & L for *High, Medium,* and *Low.*

In another column, put an H-M-L next to the "loves" that you CURRENTLY assign. For example, if your spouse or kids are an "H" but you're not spending much time with them, you might need to put an "M" or "L" next to that item.

Finally, go through each item and look at it. What "loves" do you currently classify as an "M" or "L" that you actually have the second designation as an "H"? an of these? If so, this may be a clue that you might need to re-arrange your priorities!

Check out the *Monthly Mentor Program* at *www.monthlymentorreview.com*. If you followed only this program and the *Money Matrix Method*™ - and nothing else - your life would never be the same. Your dreams would be unstoppable!

Once your have completed the work in the earlier chapters, you should be able to <u>*do what you love*</u> . . . and *only* what you love! If you have something fist designated as an "H" and you are NOT putting a High value on it currently, wake up! This is what you need to be focusing on!!

"But Michael," you might say, *"most of the 'loves' I have designated as an 'H' are things that won't bring in money."*

No? I beg to differ, and here's why . . .

What EVER you love is probably something that OTHERS love also. You may also discover that it relates to some method that DOES bring in money.

For example **Gary Vanurchuk** *loves* wine: he talks about wine all the time, and reviews wine online. While some may argue that you can't make a lot of money with wine, tell that to Mr. V who rakes in *millions* from his video blogs and affiliate products!

You have a story – the story of true love for something. Don't you think others might want to hear your story or learn your secret?

In such a case where you discover a hot market that needs your solution, I have only one piece of advice: *Tell 'em and sell 'em.*

Here's to your *Outrageous* Success!! ☺

- Dr. Michael Craig, the *"Logical Soul® Guy"*

P.S., If you are interested in Charles F. Haanel's *Master Key System*, you can get his 1912 classic as **Before the Secret**, a free E-Course you can download from www.mywealthattraction.com.

Free video training
www.moneymatrixmethod.com/bonus

Tell Your Friends
If you find this book and video training helpful, tell others about www.moneymatrixmethod.com.

Order More Books
Better yet, order 3 books and give them away to those you love, or want to do business with. They'll thank you for it! You can order more at www.incomeathomesecrets.com/books

Online Business Training
Get the complete online *Money Matrix Method*™ online business video training program at www.incomeathomespot.com

---

Glossary of Terms

Access – This is the third phase of the *Money Matrix Method™* and determines whether or not hidden decisions can be changed easily, or will require a more involved process. When Access is "available," a person's conscious mind can communicate directly with the inner decision-maker for faster results.

Archetype – A universal image, story, or relationship shared by all human beings as perceived reality. Examples of Archetypes may include the king, father, mother, child, Madonna, villain, wizard, warrior, etc.

Archetypal Matrix Decisions – These are Matrix decisions that lie beyond the "Wall" and are not accessible by the conscious mind except by obtaining Access using a more involved process.

Congruent – In alignment with: two ninety-degree angles are said to be "congruent." This term is also used to imply consistency between inner beliefs and outward statements or actions.

Cycle of Manifestation – This is the pattern that illustrates how we go from thought to results. There are two cycles, "Normal" and "Self-Sabotage." Each describes a different inner matrix.

Discovery – The second phase of the *Money Matrix Method™*, this involves getting feedback through muscle testing or some other means to establish statements that are either *congruent* or *incongruent* with the body's reactions.

Hidden Decisions – Also called "Hidden Matrix Decisions" or "HMDs" - decisions a person makes when he or she is very young, and/or under emotional or psychological stress. During such times, decisions about reality can contradict other teachings, beliefs or decisions, and are pushed into the subconscious mind, into an area where they may not be seen, but still affect outward results. Hidden decisions usually hold all the emotion surrounding that original decision, and cannot change unless or until this original decision is accessed (see *access*).

Hierarchy of Needs – A pyramid chart developed by humanistic psychologist Abraham Maslow as part of his *Theory of Motivation.* Maslow asserted that there are different levels of need, and that fundamental levels must be addressed before "higher" level needs like self-esteem or self-actualization - are met.

Incongruent – Not in alignment or agreement with (see "congruent").

Law of Attraction – The universal quality that brings to a person whatever he or she truly thinks about and holds closest to heart. The LOA also involves some underlying and little-known principles that lay out the foundation for how a person manifests results in his or her life. These are outlined in Dr. Craig's soon-to-be-published book *The Nine Hidden Laws That Can Change Your Life.*

Law of Human Reality - The principle that allows us to choose (inside) between responsibility or victimhood. Whichever we have chosen becomes the foundation of our reality and experience.

Law of the Very Good Reason – There is a very good reason for everything that happens in our lives – wanted or unwanted. If unwanted, there are deeper, hidden matrix decisions that are "switched on" that attract the negative results.

Linked Decision. A decision containing a paradox and contradiction between two "truths." One truth is known consciously and can be expressed while the other remains hidden to the conscious mind, but still expresses itself through the body, emotions, or environment. A linked decision adds struggle and suffering to your personal story.

Logical Soul® - A simple, natural technique that allows anyone to quickly discover, access, and change deeper, hidden or matrix decisions for greater freedom and awareness in all areas of life.

Logical Soul® Forgiveness Process – A simple and effective way to eliminate resentments "without letting them off the hook."

Lynchpin Decision – A key hidden decision that act as the *prime directive* for other *hidden decisions, memes,* or *meme clusters.* Changing a lynchpin decision can change a person's view of his or her existing reality.

Master Key System – Charles F. Haanel's 1912 self-development classic, a.k.a *Before the Secret.*

Meme – A unit of social information or "mind virus." A Meme is an idea, belief, or packet of information (e.g., a catchy tune) that seeks to propagate itself as quickly and widely as possible.

Meme Cluster – a collection of Memes whose sole purpose is to protect and propagate the cluster. Even if one meme is found and eliminated, the others will make sure the *prime directive* is maintained.

Money Matrix –This is your inner capacity to attract money and wealth, and the basis of your motivation to have it, or go out and get it.

Money Matrix Method™ - Method of expanding one's Money Matrix, or allowing the hidden, matrix decisions that rule one's motivation and behavior about money to be changed.

Monthly Mentor Program™ – Raymond Aaron's powerful system for finding and achieving goals in life. See www.monthlymentorreview.com for details.

Muscle Testing – A fast, easy, and readily-available form of psycho-cybernetic feedback, also called "Applied Kinesiology." This method usually involves testing the deltoid (arm-shoulder muscle) to get a weak or strong response, indicating a "false" or "true" response to a given statement or stimulus.

NLP – Neuro-linguistic programming. It is both an approach to persuasive communication using things like modeling and patterning; NLP is also a system of alternative therapy designed to raise self-awareness in communication, and change patterns of mental and emotional behavior.

No-Wealth Zone – The place where hidden decisions about money go to hide. The Money Matrix of a person who has difficulty earning or attracting money and wealth.

Personal Archetype – See Personal Story.

Personal Story –This is the narrative that forms the foundation of your purpose, motivation and behavior.

Preparation – The first phase of the Money Matrix Method. This involves laying out the purpose of the session, listening and interacting with a partner, patient or client.

Prime Directive – The programmed objective of a *meme* or *meme cluster.*

Quest – Personal story goal or dream.

Resolution – This is the fourth and final phase of the Money Matrix Method™ and involves changing the hidden decision and integrating it back into the conscious mind and body.

Santa Claus Theory of Reality – Desire leads to Results. This is the short-hand version of the "Normal Cycle of Manifestation," i.e., the way we *want* life to be, not the way it is.

Success Sabotage Syndrome – A chronic condition that prompts a person to sabotage his or her success because subconscious or deeply-rooted matrix decisions are set in place that demand higher priority.

Theory of Motivation – Abraham Maslow's classic theory, developed in the 1940's, that set out the basic factors involved in human motivation.

The Wall – The subconscious barrier that keeps hidden decisions or matrices hidden.

Win-Win – A relationship whereby both parties cooperate to gain something beneficial to each. Usually this means that the supply is perceived as unlimited, and that both parties help each other by making the resource "pie" bigger.

Zero Sum – A relationship whereby one party wins at the expense of the other. Usually this means that supply is perceived as limited, and both parties must fight over the same "pie," resource or prize.

Resources

Goals & Mindset
www.moneymatrixmethod.com – Go there!
www.logicalsoul.com – My blog
www.logicalsoultalk.com –My online radio show *Logical Soul Talk* has been airing since 2009.
www.monthlymentorreview.com – Raymond's site.
www.logicalsoul.com/products/mmformula.php - Jason Oman's incredible *Millionaire Money Formula!*

Topic Research
Find your market and your audience.
www.answers.yahoo.com
www.allexperts.com
www.askville.amazon.com

Domain Names
www.namecheap.com and www.1and1.com

Website Hosting
www.hostgator.com – The best & cheapest.
www.ixwebhosting.com

Autoresponder Service
www.aweber.com – Good service; user –friendly.
www.icontact.com – For bigger and more lists.

Product Creation
www.idictate.com – Transcription service
www.kunaki.com – Drop-ship CDs and DVDs
www.logicalsoul.com/products/flipcamerasecrets.php - Turn your Flip Camera into a high-quality studio!
www.logicalsoul.com/products/writeabook.php - Ronda del Boccio's excellent writing how-to.
www.logicalsoul.com/products/ibssecrets.php - Jason Oman's secret to launching a Best Seller!
www.logicalsoul.com/products/websiteflipping.php - How to create and sell websites fast!

www.skype.com – Free web cam calls you can record.
www.techsmith.com – Use *Camtasia* to create high-quality videos for use on websites, blogs and sales pages.
www.camstudio.org – Free video creation.

PDF Document Creation
www.pdf995.com
www.cutepdf.com

Website Creation
www.kompozer.net – Free Web design software.
www.blogger.com – Free blogs
www.wordpress.com – Free blogs and plugins.
www.filezilla-project.org – Free FTP software

Website Sales Copy
www.saleslettergenerator.com
www.pushbuttonletter.com
www.hypnoticwritingwizard.com

Outsourcing Help
www.freelabortips.com – Hire Interns for Free!
www.guru.com – advice and help on any topic.
www.freelancer.com – Virtual help on anything
www.fiverr.com – Most jobs done for only $5!

Affiliate Selling
www.amazon.com – Physical products with descriptions and reviews. Sell as an Associate
www.clickbank.com - #1 Virtual affiliate product site
www.cj.com – Commission Junction – Physical products; name brands.
www.logicalsoul.com/sam - Sam Bell's *Internet Domination System* is simply the most powerful marketing tool I've run across. This guy's a genius!
www.logicalsoul.com/products/cbwealthformula.php - *Clickbank Wealth Formula.*
www.logicalsoultalk.com/devon - Devon Brown's 27K Traffic Formula. This is the best traffic method I've seen.

Made in the USA
Charleston, SC
18 March 2012